I wish I were...

a princess

Ivan Bulloch & Diane James

WORLD BOOK / TWO-CAN

Art Director: Ivan Bulloch
Editor: Diane James
Design Assistant: Lisa Nutt
Illustrator: Dom Mansell
Photographer: Daniel Pangbourne
Models: Courtney, Natalia, Shelby, Jonathan, Grant, Kaz, Abi, Stephanie
Special thanks to: Karen Ingebretsen, World Book Publishing

Adult assistance may be necessary for some of the activities in this book.

First published in the United States and Canada by
World Book, Inc.
525 W. Monroe
Chicago, IL 60661
in association with Two-Can Publishing Ltd.

© Two-Can Publishing Ltd., 1997

**For information on other World Book products,
call 1-800-255-1750, x 2238.**

ISBN: 0-7166-5504-7 (hard cover)
ISBN: 0-7166-5505-5 (soft cover)
LC: 96-61753

Printed in Spain

1 2 3 4 5 6 7 8 9 10 01 00 99 98 97

Contents

Being a princess was very hard work, but lots of fun, too! Living in a huge stone castle could be a bit chilly, but plenty of parties with delicious food made up for that! All princesses wore beautiful gowns and loads of precious jewels. Would you like to be a princess? *Yes! Well, let's get started now. . .*

A princess had to get up extremely early in the morning. She needed lots of help to get dressed.

1 Tape the long sides of two sheets of wrapping paper together. Pleat the top edge and staple each fold in position. If you don't have a stapler, use tape.

First, she struggled into a long petticoat and a tight bodice. A richly embroidered gown went on top. You would never, ever have caught a princess wearing jeans and a T-shirt!

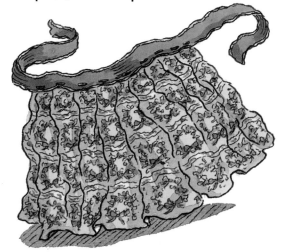

2 Finish the waist edge by stapling or gluing on a length of ribbon. The ribbon should be longer than the skirt so that you can tie it around your waist.

3 Make some bows from ribbon and fasten them to the waistband. They will cover up the tape or staples. Add brightly colored streamers to finish your skirt.

4 Cut the center hole out of a paper doily. Snip through from the middle to the outside edge. Slip the doily around your neck to make a beautiful collar.

It's not that difficult being a princess – so far!

All princesses had to wear crowns. Because crowns were usually made from solid gold, they were very heavy. To keep a crown balanced on her head, a princess had to walk with a straight back and her head held high.

1 To make sure that your crown fits perfectly, measure around your head with a tape measure or a piece of string. Add a little extra to allow for an overlap.

glue

glue

glue

2 Use the measurement you have made to cut a crown shape from posterboard. Glue the ends together.

3 Now you can decorate your crown with colored paper, candies, or shiny sequins.

This one fits perfectly – as long as I don't bend down!

If there was one thing a princess loved more than anything else in the world, it was expensive jewelry – rich, red rubies, glittering garnets, and sparkling sapphires.

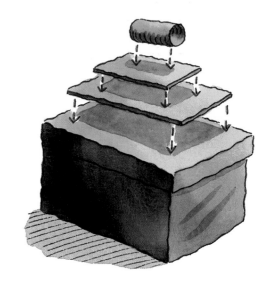

1 Find a strong cardboard box. A shoe box would be ideal. Glue two pieces of cardboard on top of the lid – one slightly smaller than the other. Glue a small cardboard roll to the top.

She could never have enough necklaces, brooches, and bangles. A special jewel box was a must for keeping everything safe.

2 Decorate the box by gluing on shapes torn, or cut, from colored paper.

I hope she likes my gift. It cost all my allowance!

3 Finish your jewel box by gluing on brightly colored candies. They won't cost a fortune but will look like real jewels.

Princesses were expected to sit on beautiful – but very uncomfortable – thrones for hours on end. They had to listen to endless speeches and greet hundreds of visitors.

How they longed for a comfortable armchair to ease their tired, aching bones. But you couldn't be a proper princess without a throne!

1 Use a sturdy stool as the base for your throne. Find a large cardboard box to fit over the stool. You may have to cut the sides of the box down a little to make it fit.

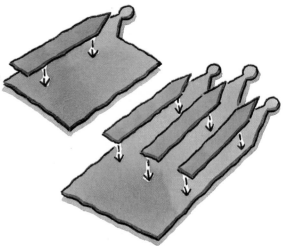

2 Cut two cardboard shapes to fit over the sides of the box, and one for the back. Decorate each of the shapes with colored paper.

3 Now glue the sides and the back in place. And most important of all, put a comfy cushion on the seat. Your throne is ready!

Time for a rest!

D uring the day a busy princess needed a break from speeches and visitors. What could be better exercise than a healthy gallop in the park? The princess chose her favorite horse and set off with her friends and pets. The cows were amazed!

1 Cut out these pieces to make a horse's head from cardboard. Paint the eye, nose, and mouth.

Hold on tight, here we go. Follow me!

Keep up and don't get left behind!

3 Glue on your horse's eye, ears, and mouth. Cut short lengths of thick string or rope and glue them on the horse's neck to make a mane.

2 Next ask a grown-up to cut a slit in the top of a broomstick, deep enough to insert your horse's head.

4 Slot the head into the slit in the broomstick. You can also put an eye and mouth on the other side of the head.

At the end of the day, when royal work was finished, the princess had time to enjoy herself.

1 To make a tambourine, cut a strip of cardboard 20 in. (50 cm) long and 3 in. (8 cm) deep. Cut three holes 2 in. (5 cm) long and 1 in. (2.5 cm) deep.

What she liked best was to listen to her favorite music. Musicians came to entertain the princess. She often joined in and sang and danced until it was time to eat!

2 Tape the ends of the cardboard strip together. Cover it with small pieces of newspaper and flour-and-water paste.

3 Collect six metal bottle tops. Ask a grown-up to make holes in them and thread through a short length of wire. Tape the wire and bottle tops to the inside of the holes. Take care with the sharp edges on the bottle tops. Cover the tape with more paste and paper.

I've never played for a princess before!

4 Paint your tambourine in bright colors and patterns. Shake it around to join in with the rest of the band!

When the music was over, the princess had a delicious meal with all her friends. Nobody bothered to use knives and forks – fingers were fine! Royal pets joined in and helped chew on the bones. Drinks were served in jeweled goblets.

1 Find some plastic or paper cups. Cut out circles from cardboard to make bases for your goblets. Glue the cups to the bases.

2 Paint rich, jewel-like patterns on the outside of your goblets. Acrylic paints will work best on plastic cups. Don't try to drink out of your goblets, just pretend!

Three cheers for the band and all my friends!

O n special occasions a princess really enjoyed attending an exciting jousting tournament. Handsome knights on horseback charged and tried to knock each other off! The princess cheered loudly for her favorite horseman.

I've got a feeling that I'm going to win today

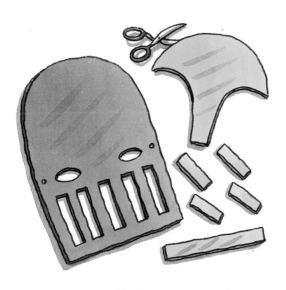

1 Cut out all the pieces for your knight's helmet from colored posterboard. Make holes for the eyes and long, narrow slits so you can breathe and shout out loud!

2 Glue on the pieces of posterboard. Make small holes on either side. Thread cord through. Knot the ends so they don't slip through.

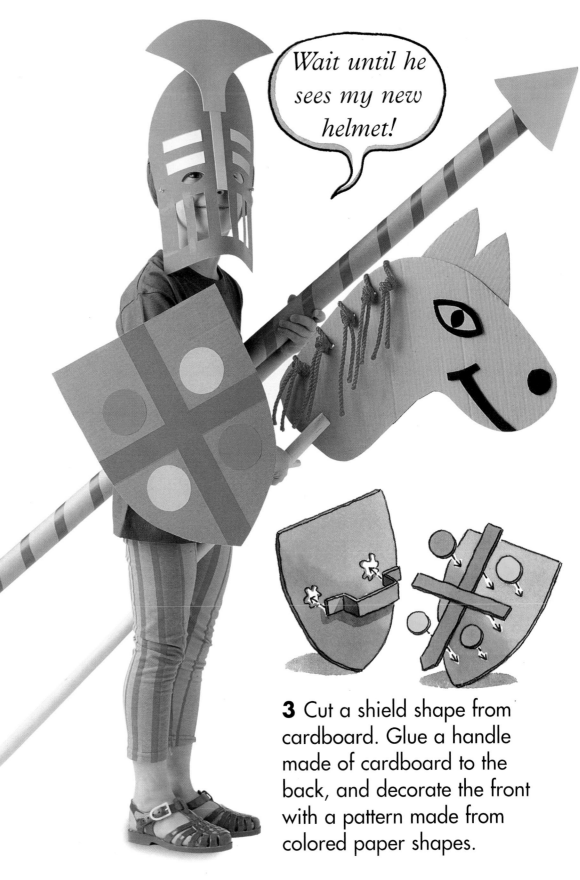

Wait until he sees my new helmet!

3 Cut a shield shape from cardboard. Glue a handle made of cardboard to the back, and decorate the front with a pattern made from colored paper shapes.

Every princess dreamed of sharing her life with a handsome, brave husband. The wedding gave everyone in the royal palace a good excuse for holding a huge party to celebrate. The musicians played, the court jester joked with the guests, and the cook prepared a massive banquet. It was the best day the princess had ever had in her life!

Come and join in the fun.

And EVERYONE lived very happily ever after!

P rincesses sometimes used words that would sound very strange today! Here are just a few to help you carry on a royal conversation.

I pardon you with all my heart...

OK, I forgive you.

Trouble not yourself about that...

Don't worry, it'll be all right!

I am sure some mischance will befall us...

We could be in trouble!

Why, how now, good mother...

Hi, Mom!

You have been long in coming...

Why are you so late?